Things in Springtime

Illustrated by
Di Brookes

Designed by Jenny Addison and Helen Cooke
Words by Lara Bryan and Kate Nolan

There's a chart with stickers at the back of the book
to help you keep track of the things you have seen.

Parks

Male blackbird
(females are
brown)

Blackbird

Look for it hopping around
lawns with its head cocked
to one side, listening for
earthworms. Keep an ear
out for its beautiful song.

Red mason bee

This small bee likes to
nest in the crumbling
mortar of old walls.

Covered in
gingery hair

Crocus

These purple, orange, white or
yellow flowers pop up on lawns
from February to April. They're
a sign spring is on its way.

Beetles feed on the flower's tasty pollen.

Magnolia tree

Its large flowers bloom in shades of pink and white on bare branches before the leaves have grown.

Chiffchaff

You might hear this tiny bird singing its name – 'chiff chaff chiff chaff' – from the treetops.

Orange-tip butterfly

One of the earliest butterflies to hatch. Only the males have orange wingtips.

Gardens

Great tit

Look out for it chasing off smaller birds at birdtables to get to the food. Its song sounds like 'tea-cher, tea-cher'.

Holly blue butterfly

From April, you'll find these butterflies fluttering over gardens and hedgerows.

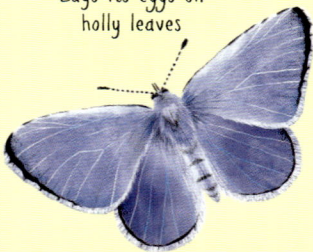

Lays its eggs on holly leaves

Daffodil

Spot patches of these trumpet-like flowers in different shades of yellow and orange from February to May.

Apple tree

Sweetly-scented blossom coats the branches in shades of pink and white. The apples won't be ready until later in the summer.

Hedgehog

If you're lucky, you might spot one snuffling around after sunset when it comes out to feast on insects.

Covered in over 5,000 spines

Green lacewing

These lime-green insects patrol up and down leaves munching on tiny green or brown bugs called aphids.

Woodlands

Hawthorn tree

In May, these trees are covered in creamy white blossom. By autumn, they'll be full of bright red berries.

Wild garlic

The garlicky smell of the leaves is hard to miss! From April, look for this plant in damp, dark places.

Bluebell

You might see clusters of these bell-shaped flowers in shady woodlands from April to May.

Males have red patches
on their heads.

Great spotted woodpecker

Rat-a-tat-tat... you'll probably
hear this bird before you see it.
It pecks at trees to catch insects,
communicate and hollow out
nests for their chicks.

The spots on its wings
look like eyes.

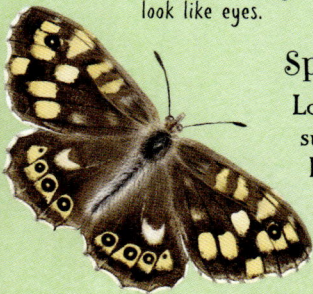

Speckled wood butterfly

Look out for it fluttering through
sunny patches of woodland.
It will often chase away other
butterflies from its territory.

Wood anemone

At the start of spring, these star-shaped
flowers race to grow before the
tree branches fill up with leaves
and block out the light.

Woodlands

Bullfinch

Tread quietly and you might spot this shy bird's bright pink-red feathers as it collects twigs and moss for its nest.

Hazel tree

Look for its flowers in early spring, followed by round, green leaves. Come back in autumn for tasty nuts.

Its flowers are called catkins.

Lily of the valley

Its white flowers are shaped like little bells. Green, glossy leaves carpet the ground in May and June.

Cuckoo

These birds arrive in spring and lay their eggs in other birds' nests. Listen out for their 'cuck-oo' call.

So small it can fit in a matchbox

Pipistrelle bat

If you're close to water on a warm evening, you might glimpse one darting about hunting for insects.

Wood sorrel

Small white flowers peep out above heart-shaped leaves from April to May. They often grow from moss on fallen logs.

Fields and Farmlands

Calf

You'll find calves nibbling on grass in farmers' fields. Keep a good distance from them and their mothers.

Has black-tipped ears

Brown hare

Watch out for hares bounding in a zig-zag pattern across fields. Larger than a rabbit, with longer legs and ears.

Chick

After hatching, fluffy yellow chicks keep close to their mother for food and warmth.

Skylark

This streaky brown bird swoops and hovers over fields, trilling and warbling from up high.

Its coat is softer than an adult sheep.

Lamb

Around farms, look out for fields full of playful lambs waggling their tails as they drink their mother's milk.

Cowslip

These small tube-like flowers cluster at the top of tall green stems.

Moors and Meadows

White-tailed bumblebee

This fuzzy bee has a bright white tail and feeds on wildflowers all spring and summer long.

Early purple orchid

Look out for the purply splodges on its leaves. Each plant can have up to fifty pinkish-purple flowers.

Bracken

One of the most ancient and widespread plants around the world. Each spring, new fronds uncurl into long stems of feathery leaves.

Fritillary

If you're lucky, you might find a patch of these unusual, chequered flowers growing in a damp meadow.

Gorse

Its bright yellow flowers smell of coconuts. Many birds shelter among the sharp, spiky branches in rainy and windy weather.

Also known as a maybug

Cockchafer

This large beetle buzzes loudly as it flies. Adults hatch in May and only live for six weeks.

Hedgerows

Common banded hoverfly

It looks a bit like a wasp – but it only has two wings and doesn't sting. Try and spot it hovering in the air.

Common dog violet

Find these delicate purple flowers with heart-shaped leaves growing close to the ground from April to June.

Primrose

In early spring, look out for this creamy yellow flower nestled at the bottom of hedgerows. Its name comes from the words for 'first rose' in Latin.

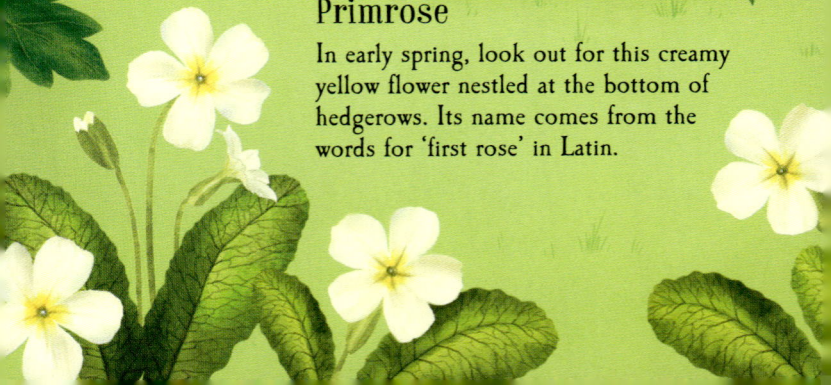

Blackthorn tree

In spring, its branches are covered in clouds of feathery white blossom. If you come back in the autumn, you'll see its inky blue fruits (sloes).

Lesser celandine

If you're on a damp shady path, keep a lookout for these flowers with their glossy heart-shaped leaves.

Hawthorn shieldbug

See if you can spot the green shield on its back framed by reddish sides. It likes to nibble on hawthorn leaves.

15

Ponds and lakes

Common toad

Look for these in the evening, when they come out to slurp up tasty slugs and snails.

Warty skin and copper eyes

Males have a crest running down their backs.

Smooth newt

This spotty creature is about the length of an adult's finger. They go to ponds to breed in spring.

Marsh marigold

These large golden flowers pop up in wet places from March onwards.

Mallard

Watch for fluffy mallard ducklings swimming close to their mother – they might have hatched that same day.

Common frog

Frogs often return to the same pond every spring to mate and lay eggs. Look out for their patchy backs and stripy legs.

Lays up to 5,000 eggs in one go

Large red damselfly

You might spot this damselfly zooming over ponds from late April. Has a bright red body with black markings.

Catches insects mid-air

17

Rivers and canals

Swallow

From early spring, look out for swallows swooping across the sky or darting to their nests under roofs.

Speeds through the air hunting insects

Cuckooflower

Clusters of cuckooflowers pop up in damp, grassy meadows and riverbanks. Flowers are pink or white with four petals.

Builds floating nests out of water grasses

Coot

Look for the white 'shield' above its beak. It dives down deep to catch insects.

Weeping willow

Its long branches sweep down to the ground and make good nesting sites for birds.

Long, pointy leaves

Swan

Glides majestically across water. You might spot it bottom up, reaching down with its long neck to feed on weeds and insects.

Carries its young on its back

Hairy dragonfly

These speedy dragonflies can hover and even fly backwards. If one stays still for long enough, you might see its hairy underside.

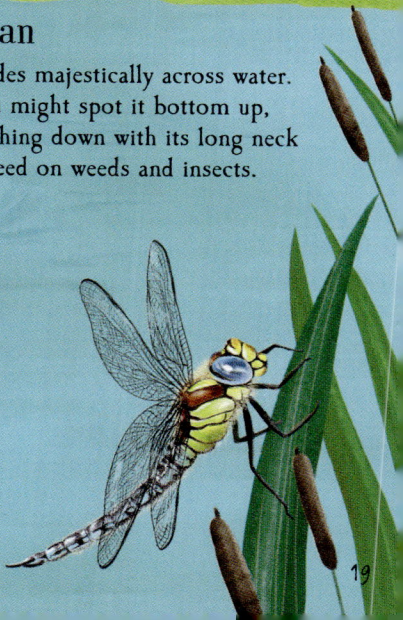

Towns and cities

Cherry tree

Blossoms for just a week or two in March or April – so catch it while you can!

Flowers smell of almonds

Tulip

One of the most popular garden flowers. There are thousands of different varieties, with petals that can be stripy, pointy or even frilly.

Dandelion

Very easy to spot – it can grow almost anywhere. After it flowers, fluffy white seedheads grow and scatter in the wind.

Swift

Spends most of its life flying
– even sleeping in the air.
In the sky, seen from down
below, it looks black.

Has a
forked tail

Fox

Mainly comes out at
night to forage for worms,
beetles and any leftover
food it can find.

Adults bring food back to
the den for their cubs.

Hyacinth

In March and April look for
them flowering in plant pots,
on window sills or in the ground.
Smells fresh and sweet.

Spotting chart

Once you've spotted something from this book, find its sticker at the back, and stick it on this chart in the space below its name.

Apple tree	Blackbird	Blackthorn tree	Bluebell	Bracken
Brown hare	Bullfinch	Calf	Cherry tree	Chick
Chiffchaff	Cockchafer	Common banded hoverfly	Common dog violet	Common frog
Common toad	Coot	Cowslip	Crocus	Cuckoo
Cuckooflower	Daffodil	Dandelion	Early purple orchid	Fox

Fritillary	Gorse	Great spotted woodpecker	Great tit	Green lacewing
Hairy dragonfly	Hawthorn shieldbug	Hawthorn tree	Hazel tree	Hedgehog
Holly blue butterfly	Hyacinth	Lamb	Large red damselfly	Lesser celandine
Lily of the valley	Magnolia tree	Mallard	Marsh marigold	Orange-tip butterfly
Pipistrelle bat	Primrose	Red mason bee	Skylark	Smooth newt
Speckled wood butterfly	Swallow	Swan	Swift	Tulip
Weeping willow	White-tailed bumblebee	Wild garlic	Wood anemone	Wood sorrel

Index

First published in 2025 by Usborne Publishing Limited, 83–85 Saffron Hill, London EC1N 8RT, United Kingdom. usborne.com
Copyright © 2025 Usborne Publishing Limited. The name Usborne and the Balloon logo are trade marks of Usborne Publishing Limited. All rights reserved. No part of this publication may be reproduced, stored in a retrieval system or transmitted in any form or by any means without the prior permission of the publisher. Printed in China. UKE.